MRS GOD

MRS GOD

AND OTHER POEMS

BY

TOM STAMP

CAEDMON OF WHITBY

By the same author: A Pocketful of Rhyme
Poems From Whitby
Miss Raine's Flowers
Whitby in Winter
Collected Whitby Poems
A Meeting of Minds
William Scoresby
Captain Cook

1SBN 0 905355 40 7

Typeset by Proprint, Whitby
Printed by Smith Settle, Otley
Published by Caedmon of Whitby, 128 Upgang Lane,
Whitby, North Yorkshire.

Never say with grief: He is no more,
But rather say with thankfulness: He was.

CONTENTS

INTRODUCTION

As all poets know, the making of a poem is not an easy task.
It seldom was for my husband, and in going through his papers
I have found many versions of the same poem copied out over
and over again with perhaps one word altered here and there.
I ask the reader's indulgence in many of the poems which were
unfinished at his death which to a practised eye may appear to
need polishing.
There were so many bright gems among them that I felt it right
to include them.

W.B. Yeats knew about it:

> *I said, "A line will take us hours maybe,*
> *Yet if it does not seem a moment's thought*
> *Our stitching and unstitching has been naught.*
> *Better go down upon your marrow bones*
> *And scrub a kitchen pavement, or break stones*
> *Like an old pauper in all kinds of weather;*
> *For to articulate sweet sounds together*
> *Is to work harder than all these, and yet*
> *Be thought an idler by the noisy set*
> *Of bankers, schoolmasters and clergymen*
> *The martyrs call the world."*

The great Russian writer, Konstantin Paustovsky, wrote of Poetry:

I was swept along by it as irresistibly as a branch broken from a tree is swept by a torrent. I saw everything through the transparent medium of poetry. . . . I have never for a moment regretted having been possessed by poetry in my youth because now I know that poetry is life. Life carried to its maximum power of expression. It is the world revealed in its fullest depths, a depth never revealed to the indolent eye.

The final quotation is by Tom's greatest mentor, William Wordsworth, in a letter to Sir George Beaumont:

" . . . . . . Thanks for dear Lady Beaumont's transcript from your friend's letter. It is written with candour, but I must say a word or two not in praise of it.

"Instances of what I mean," says your friend, "are to be found in a poem on a Daisy" (By the by, it is on THE Daisy, a mighty difference) "and in Daffodils reflected in water."

Is this accurately transcribed by Lady Beaumont? If it is, what shall we think of criticism or judgment founded upon and exemplified by a poem which must have been so inattentively perused?!

My language is precise, and therefore it would be false modesty to charge myself with blame.

> *Ten thousand saw I at a glance*
> *Tossing their heads in sprightly dance*
> *The waves beside them danced,*
> *But they outdid the sparkling waves in glee.*

Can expression be more distinct?

And let me ask your friend, how is it possible for flowers to be reflected in water when there are waves? They may be indeed in still water, but the very object of my poem is the trouble or agitation of the flowers and of the water.

I must needs respect the understanding of everyone honoured by your friendship - but sincerity compels me to say that my poems must be more nearly looked at before they can give rise to any remarks of much value, even from the strongest minds . . . What then shall we say? Why, let the poet first consult his own heart as I have done and leave the rest to posterity. To, I hope, an improving posterity . . . in short, in your friend's letter I am condemned for the very thing which I ought to have been praised, viz: that I have not written down to the level of superficial observers and unthinking minds.

Every great poet is a teacher, and I would wish to be considered as a Teacher or as nothing."

Parkinson's disease took its inexorable toll of my husband, among other things hand writing became difficult and then impossible and one or two of his later scribbles are very hard to decipher. The only comfort was that the disease hardly affected his mind, which remained clear to the very end. So let me close with his own words written during his last days:

". . . The only other worthwhile human activities are music, literature, poetry and art, which enhance the beauty and dignity of life and aid in the fight against vulgarity in all its forms."

> *Man is the only creature*
> *Here on earth*
> *Who seeks a mass destruction*
> *Of his kind.*
> *Why so wilful and so blind?*
> *He who gave birth*
> *To music, art and the ceaseless*
> *Venturing of the creative mind . . .*

Cordelia Stamp

Whitby 1993

MRS GOD

No one tells us about Mrs God
I bet she's the power behind the
throne
He couldn't live all alone
Up there
Someone would have to share
His Kingdom
No one's complete without a spouse
And the house
Of many mansions
Needs a womans hand
As every home.
How could even God roam
Through countless rooms
Endlessly and for ever ?

MR GOD'S LAMENT

I look with sorrow down below
At all I started long ago
And see that all my splendid schemes
Were only sad, romantic dreams.
The plans had quite a lovely shape
With such a gentle, guileless ape,
But all went wrong. I know not why.
I think it was this lonely sky,
So vast, so empty, so remote.

I often tried to intervene,
But there was such a gap between.
Perhaps with less to see and do
I might have had a better view
And kept things working with more skill.
But then I was quite often ill,
The suns and stars and nebulae
Drained all my energies away.
And now I find in Moon and Mars
That man moves nearer to the stars.
Who knows! I may meet face to face
This wrecker of celestial space.
For now I see that Mr Man
Sets out to shape a wiser plan.
With careful steps both firm and strong,
He seeks to show where I went wrong.
With D.N.A. and boundless space
He tries to build a better place.

I wish him luck with all my heart,
For I am ready to depart,
And Mrs God this many a day
Has said that we are fools to stay,
" Let's start a Mission down in Hell,
Im sure the plan would go quite well!"

This house of many mansions bores
With all its shining pearly doors.
I'd rather have a cosy den
Outside the universe of MEN!

Lets start another universe
Without this dreadful human curse.
Just plants and mice and furry creeping things
And lovely birds with shining wings,
With whales and snails and snow white bears,
And make them all in perfect pairs,
To live and love and innocent lie,
Beneath the all-embracing sky.
Then worries over ways of men
Would fade for ever from our ken!

SIMPLE GOODNESS

Conventionally religious people distress me.
They are so often humourless, so deadly
Serious. Seeing the hand of God in
Everything should make them glow
Like sunsets, blossom like may trees,
Burgeon with beauty and wonder
And praise.
Instead of which they spend
Their days much as others do.
Only they don't seem to get
Much fun out of it.

But sometimes simple goodness
Shines through and familiar words
Take on fresh meaning, and then
People who go about
Preening themselves
In the public eye
Seem unimportant.

PRAYER

I feel I know
Where e'er I go
That there will always be
A world of wonder waiting there
To fold and comfort me,
For ever since I walked the world
I've sought to find
How it unfurled,
And why its strange, yet lovely, face
Would meet me in some quiet place.
So when towards the end of day
The sunlit clouds their form display,
Then do I often quietly pray
And thank whatever gods there be
That I can hear, and feel and see.

CHRISTMAS 1970

Draw close up to the fireside,
Forget the world, just for one day,
And keep this Christmas in your heart
The festive and the friendly way.
For what the world most surely needs
Is folk secure in hearth and home
Who never far from either roam,
And yet who give to friends and kin
An ever joyful welcoming.

For like a glowing Christmas tree
That puts a magic in a room,
His love can make your spirit shine
And chase away all fear and gloom.

The child that came at Christmas time
To stable stall with feeble cries
Is Lord of all the earth and skies,
And ever shall His truth shine bright, -
Only love can set the world aright.

GREY DAYS

The pewter sky leans, rainfilled
On the rutted field . . .

(Photograph by Bill Shaw)

GREY DAYS

I like grey days
When the harsh bright
Outlines of the busy world
Are softened and subdued
By morning mist
And trees in country lanes
Loom mysterious
As you pass them by
The pewter sky leans
Rainfilled
On the rutted field
I feel my spirit yield
To the quietness and calm
A solitary soul walking
All unseeing
At the centre of his being
Through the misty air
What can compare
With such soul-soothing
Solitude?
Give me grey days
And quiet lonely ways
I ask no more

CHRISTMAS 1968

An age ago he came
To show all men the power of love.
And a few simple souls followed
In his path.
But the rest did naught but laugh
And let greed and power and military might
Be their way to set the world aright.
And they've been doing it ever since.
He was sent to show the way,
But they have bent and twisted
All he had to say.
But still the simple truth shines bright,
Only love can set the world aright.

GOD IS EVERYWHERE

God is everywhere in creation,
At the centre and on the rim,
He is everything
And everything is in Him.
He is the one and the many,
The child laughing,
And the daffodil,
The look of love
The way of wonder,
The mood of mystery,
The meaning of all history,
The rapture of a moment's bliss.

MRS UG'S ADVICE

Don't look out of the cave, my dear,
You don't know what you might see.
Better build up the fire, my dear,
And keep me company.
The man next cave looked out one day
And followed a tiger's trail,
He's not been seen again, my dear,
She told me a dreadful tale
Of how she saw the tiger turn
And eat him in a trice,
You'd better by far stay here, my dear,
The story's not very nice.
The people who go abroad I fear
Seldom if ever return.
Still, if you think you might get a new fur wrap
You could go out for a while.
But don't go as far as the Dinosaur bar,
And come back here for tea.
Then you could finish your paintings, my dear,
The wall looks better by far!

HARVEST THANKSGIVING

Come ye thankful people come,
Make contributions one by one.
Air tickets must be bought,
Archbishops to the sunshine brought.

Winter chills and winter snow
Must not on Bishops come or go.
So rally round and see that they
From winter ills are safe away.

All is safely gathered in,
Let the archbishops' tours begin.
Canterbury to Bermuda go,
York to Dallas and Buffalo,
Archdeacons by the score
To winter sports in Baltimore.

HUMILITY

Every season we may find
Has beauty of a different kind,
And if we live beneath her spell,
Then Nature in our hearts may dwell.

For we are part of Nature's plan
And we should live within her span,
Never doing injury
To any living thing we see.

For we are conscious of our place
And so are touched by God's good grace.
Remember this in all we see
And walk with true humility.

VIEWS ON NEWS

The world is full of too much news,
Of radio and TV views,
Of commentators by the score
Who make more turmoil than before,
And turn each trivial, mundane fact
Into a huge and menacing act
Which looms so large within our day,
It makes the world seem dull and grey.

In every ear at breakfast time,
The news is poured like so much slime.
At tea and supper too
The news is there, with ringside view.
People who'd never be irate
Collect in crowds and Demonstrate;
And tribesmen in far-off lands
Amass in large and murderous bands
And decimate the status quo,
Because the radio told them so.

And all the world's stupendous sin
To each small ear is pouring in.
It is in its own curious way
Like going to funerals every day.
I think if we had more of laughter
And less of news, both now and after,
The world would be a saner place
And wear a brighter, calmer face.

For what do all these newshounds do,
But give us a most jaundiced view
Of the world in which we live?
Miss out all the joy and fun,
The kindness and the good that's done,

Harping on the crude,
The bad, the vulgar and the rude;
All the crime and sin and greed;
Every foul and dirty deed;

Murders here and shootings there;
All the terror everywhere.
Poor simple souls get so bemused,
Conscience-striken and confused,
They start to think the world is mad
And see no joy in anything.
Not even in the voice of spring,
Not even in a sunny day
Or an innocent child at play.

The world has always had its share
Of ugliness and dark despair.
But why invite into your home
The whole of it from Leeds to Rome,
From Moscow to the south of Spain,
From Ecuador and back again.
From poor Peru and Pakistan,
From Istanbul and far Japan?

You have enough to live your life,
To cherish home and love your wife,
To care for friends and neighbours too,
And all the folk that work with you.
And if you did that to perfection
You'd have no time for world inspection.

Now if throughout the world this view
Were acted on and held as true,
Then love and peace were so abundant
That newsmen all would be redundant!

CONSERVATION YEAR. 1970

Pollution of the air and stream
Proceeds apace like some bad dream.
Such carelessness and unconcern!
It seems that man will never learn
How precious is this Mother Earth
That brought him life and gave him birth,
Has nurtured him through all the years,
And now is sad with many tears,
And looks aghast with sorrowed face
While man throws filth about the place.

Man must learn to be
At one with real humanity.
For he is part of Nature's plan,
Was given form and made a man,
And if he wilfully annoys,
Pollutes, contaminates, burns, destroys,
She will discard him out of hand.
Return him to the shapeless land
From which he came but yester-year,
So full of hope, and joy and fear.

But fear of God has now declined.
Man thinks he sees, though he is blind.
Compared with what there is to know

His knowledge is a flake of snow
That glitters for a little space
And then dissolves without a trace.
If he with humility could scan
His narrow glimpse of Nature's plan
Then he might find a blessed way
To walk within the light of day.

THE SHAMING OF THE TRUE

Oh clever strutters on our present stage,
Who 'produce' Shakespeare and his friends enrage,
What arrogance to think that you
'Improve' on him in what you do.
As well bring candles in to light the sun
Or think to claim the prize before the race is run.
So much the piece is turned around
That even Shakespeare's magic can't be found.

WISDOM

The realm of science is wide and bright
And loving truth is surely right.
But wisdom comes from loving God
And walking where our Saviour trod.
Without him all will go astray
For only he can show the way.

Is this just a pious thought?
A platitude that comes to naught?
Something repeated year by year,
That never to the truth draws near?
Or is it wisdom, deep, profound,
That in the living may be found?

IN KING'S COLLEGE CHAPEL

Here the soul takes flight,
And filled with sound and light
The mind dwells in regions clear and bright.
See those windows filled with saints
And visionary souls,
The fan shaped roof,
High majestic and remote,
Fit to support the very ante-chamber
Of heaven itself.
To worship here and not be moved
Is unthinkable.
I'd just as soon be proved
An infidel . . . or worse!
As organ and choir
Vibrate the solemn air,
This moment brings my spirit
To a calm and quiet place
Where dwells a measure of that inward grace
Known only when the soul is touched
By sacred things.

16

ARMISTICE DAY, 1982

This century is worn away,
Two more decades and it has passed.
What lessons have the people learnt,
What brighter hopes of peace to last?

Two major wars have left their mark
In broken lives and bitter grief,
And some prepare for yet a third,
Although it seems beyond belief.

I know not what the years may bring
When jingo-marchers stride abroad,
And fear clouds over brighter hopes,
The plough shares rust beneath the sword.

One hopes that sense may yet prevail,
Though history shows how seldom so.
When lawless men bestride the world
Then honest men to war must go.

Have faith that men may brothers be,
And till the soil for daily bread,
For faith and work are better far
Than countless thousands lying dead.

DELIGHT

Let us look for beauty while we may
And seek to see some every day
For we should have the saddest view
Of this strange world
If we all knew
Had come to us through daily news
Of radio and TV views
A daily draught of pure delight
Will help to keep our spirits bright

The splendid open shining sky,
The river sweeping swiftly by
With flashing waters flowing wide
And sunlight like a flame inside -
The tracery green of spreading boughs,
The crystal that the earth endows
With hidden fire and coloured light
Like stars that shine from out the night,
The alchemy of earth that glows
In daffodil and summer rose,
The first green-showing shoots of spring,
The joy that kindly actions bring,
The happiness in words of praise
That help to lighten lonely days.

Let not our lives grow less and less
Through dwelling on unhappiness
Nor shrink to quite a dismal size
Because we will not use our eyes
Not just the eyes of outward sense
But the inner eye of innocence

For beauty lives in simple things
And joys beyond the wealth of kings
If we would only look and see
The beauty of simplicity.
So look for beauty while you may
And try to find some every day
Looking with kindly eyes
On all the good that round us lies
And as we go along our way
Remember to be glad and gay,
A little whimsical and kind
To others' faults a trifle blind,
Then we may grow benign and wise
And folk will see it in our eyes
Know we mean to do our best
And leave in other hands the rest.

THE TELEPHONE

Ring ring. Drat the thing.
There it goes again.
The telephone's an awful thing
And such a dreadful strain.
It rings at night. It rings at day.
It rings at home. It rings away.
I'd like to wring its neck some day.
And make subscribers one and all
Get any number but their call.

The telephone is very rude.
It never hesitates to intrude.
Where e'er you are, what e'er you do
The telephone discomforts you.
The only time it's any use
Is if a burglar's in the house.
Then you dial nine, nine, nine
And get a bobby on the line.
Then your life history he'll demand
Before he lifts his heavy hand.

The awful bore you used to meet
Occasionally along the street.
Now rings up at awkward hours.
His raucous voice it overpowers.
You used to dodge him when you could
By being busy 'doing good'.
But now the phone rings loud and clear.

Do what you will, you've got to hear.
And to his importuning ways
You can but listen with amaze.

But telephones are really vile
When you've been in the bath awhile.
They ring and ring and won't take no.
So down the stairs you've got to go.
You get quite close, seeing red,
When suddenly the thing goes dead.
And then you curse the unlucky day
The telephone came in to stay.
And say that you of all men would be least offended
If telephones were all suspended.

WASTE PAPER

*(County Hall advertised for tenders to remove
waste paper from their office.)*

First I must commence by begging your pardon
For mentioning these screeds of unintelligible jargon,
But they collect in such a wild profusion
That County Hall is covered with confusion,
So they must tender in the public press
For someone to relieve them of this mess.
Perhaps they will be turned into cartons
For fish fingers,
Whereon the smell of fish,
But not the jargon, lingers.

HOME

The simple house was very small
Yet cold and cheerless never,
To me more fine than finest hall
And dearer is it ever.

Our mother filled it with her care
And it was bright and homely
And no one was unwanted there
Or ever left or lonely.

The house was down a little yard
And up some steps two doors away,
And life was poor and often hard
Yet mother could be gay.

Our father led a sea-going life,
An iron man though tender,
And he cared deeply for his wife
To protect and to defend her.

Her courage never, never failed
Though Father came home blinded,
She carried on as if he sailed
And she had never minded.

To keep the family out of debt
She went to work for others
And had a smile for all she met,
The very best of mothers.

HOME

The Little girl who grew up to become the mother of Tom Stamp.

(Photograph by F.M. Sutcliffe)

Nor did she ever say a word,
To others left explaining,
No sorrow from her lips was heard,
No bitterness or complaining.

Yet he was sad and full of grief
That she should have to go,
And she was sad beyond relief
That he should have it so.

Then there came the happy week
When we boys earned some pay,
And Mother had no need to seek
For floors to scrub each day.

And these were times long since passed
Yet I'll forget them never,
As long as memory shall last,
A bond that none can sever.

For these my parents were to me
People sincere and rare,
With grace and simple dignity
And love beyond compare.

CHAINED MALE

In days of old the armour bright
Encased a man secure and tight.
It was a status symbol bold
That gleamed with such a steely cold
And frosty faced light.
As he went forth to a feudal furore
(Which now is part of England's story)
And created havoc with much pleasantry,
Aided and abetted by the peasantry.
And Lady Godiva gave such treats
By riding in Coventry's crowded streets,
Now modern man obtains from there
An 'overcoat' beyond compare.
Or so he thinks - poor simple fool.
But really he is just a tool.
He doesn't wear his armour new,
The armour 'wears' him - I think that's true.
And in this steely coat he speeds,
Creating havoc and ill deeds
Accompanied by incessant noise
That frays the nerves and kills all joys.
And mowing down the peasantry
With lack of feudal pleasantry.

Or if he doesn't mow them down
He gives them bronchials in the town,
And sends them to an early grave
Without being good, or bold, or brave.
There is no doubt that he must find
New armour of a different kind,
In which he moves from place to place
With dignity and simple grace.

WHITBY TOWN

Whitby town is an ancient town
Near a wide and sandy shore,
And ships have sailed from the little port
A thousand years or more-
Since the time the longboats roamed the seas
And the Norsemen went to war.
And folk have come from the lonely moors
Down to the sheltering town
With its Abbey dear, and the old church near,
And the steps up the steep hillside;
Where the gentle flow of the river below
Meets the surge of the incoming tide
Between old, stone piers
That have rung to the cheers
For the whalers coming home;
And heard angry cries at the press-gang spies
In the days of long ago.
The place where Hilda, grave, serene,
Held her gentle sway
And Caedmon sang his sacred songs
In the far-off yesterday.
The town where Cook came down to the sea
To learn his seaman's skill.
Where he kindled the flame of his splendid fame
That burns more brightly still;
For here were built those sturdy ships,
Those ships of high renown,
That brought us fame and a lasting name,
Who dwell in Whitby town.

From here the Scoresbys - father and son,-
Went off to the Greenland seas
To hunt for whale, in the days of sail
When Whitby town was a whaling town,
And second to none was she;
For the haunting shade of the bold Kinraid
Still lingers down by the sea.
Gone are the monks, and the Norsemen too,
Gone are the whaling days:
But Whitby's still a thriving place,
And proud of her ancient ways.
Poets and painters and writers too,
Have fallen under her spell,
For Whitby binds us to herself-
We folk who love her well.

THE COMING OF HILDA

Long, long ago when folk were few
And Whitby strand was bleak and bare,
There came a lady, tall and fair,
Of royal blood, commanding air
And Christian zeal beyond compare,
Striding with band of maids and men
Beside a wild and salt-sea fen
That bounded the shore on the easterly side,
And rose, reed-filled, with the rising tide,
Towards no castle or stately hall,
But the lonely hamlet of Streonshalh;
Where a lonely fishermen stood with wondering awe
To see such folk upon the shore.
And later. when their purpose known,
His craft and skill won for their own,
He oft with feeling blessed the day
When the lady Hilda came that way,
And by the power of a royal will
Transformed the lonely, wind-swept hill
Into a haven of peace and prayer
Sustained by work and wisdom there.

By sea from Hartlepool she came,
To found a monastery whose fame,
In six short years spread far and wide,
Able to nurture and provide
For all the folk in the countryside,
And be no less a royal place.
Blessed by a Synod's special grace.

For Hilda in those lawless days
Led folk beyond their pagan ways,
Making an ardent Christian life
Above the turmoil and the strife,

Showing how harvests of land and sea
Could fortify true piety,
A dignity of work and prayer
That gave to life a purposed air,
That turned men's thoughts from war and greed
To compass truly human need.

And though long years have rolled away
Since Hilda walked on Whitby strand,
Still is her name on every hand,
While those who burnt her Abbey down
Are nameless vandals lost in time,
Remembered only for a crime.

TV DIATRIBE

The TV is an ugly thing
That lurks in houses every night.
It dulls the senses, dims the sight,
And fills the air with cold green light.
The friendly chap who used to call
Is hardly ever seen all,
The neighbours who were once so kind,
Are hid behind their lowered blind.
Meals are eaten in the gloom
And family life has met its doom.
All the street's shut in with telly.
And no one cares for poor sad Nellie
Who's old and blind and rather deaf
And used to get such help for living
From neighbours who were always giving.
But now the Telly's come to stay
Poor Nellie rues the dreadful day.
I think it would be really splendid
If Telly shows were all suspended!

WENDENS AMBO

Shall we take the bridle path to Wendens Ambo?
What sort of a place will it be?
A forlorn row of faceless houses;
A petrol station with green stamps free:
Leather jacketed louts and concrete roundabouts;
Dusty bushes and rushes in flooded fields:
Hoardings making their sordid appeals,
Bingo, beer and cigarettes.
Let's leave Wendens Ambo - and no regrets.

Shall we take the bridle path to Wendens Ambo?
What sort of a place will it be?
A sleepy village, free from the noise of cars;
Dark at night so the stars shine down.
The nearest town some thirty miles away
The Wendens Ambo folk don't stay there long,
They like their rural solitude and domesticity.
What's it really like at Wendens Ambo?
We shall never know. Because we didn't go!

BLAKE IN REGENTS PARK 1973

Fearful tiger caged in steel,
What sadness must your strange heart feel,
What visions of the open plain,
Of forest glades not seen again,
What terror bring to that crude man
Who shut you in this narrow span,
Who set you pacing to and fro,
Who through the open world should go?
Those eyes that peer through narrow bars
Should blaze beneath the southern stars,
Should look through green tunnels of delight
And shine in 'forest of the night'

31

COUNTERCHARGE

Shut the door with undisguised delight.
Shoot the bolts and make the shutters tight.
Put out the light. That fellow's coming up the street.
To bar the door to him will be a treat.
All day long they come relentless through the door
For nails and screws and 'things' they've had before.
"You used to stock it. I've had it here I know."
Something he bought here twenty years ago!
But now the shop lies still and grey,
Exhausted by the effort of the day.
The till sheets neatly coiled and lying snug.
The windows covered by a steamy fug.
Plastic shapes hang strangely in the air,
And metal monsters loom in shadowy lair.
The great god mammon settles for the night.
Waiting till morning to resume the fight.
So let's away and leave him in his den.
We shop assistants are but simple men.
To pay the rent and keep the wolf at bay,
That's the reason why we work here day by day.

ANOTHER ENCOUNTER IN A SHOP

" Have you got a T Coil?" he said
What on earth can that be, thought I.
Perhaps electrical or Hi Fi?
T hinges, T cloths, T pots we sell
But T Coil doesn't ring a bell.
He stood there mute and self-contained.
Not one hint did he offer,
Nor any explanation proffer.
There was no light between
Nor any explanation seen.
And so in cold despair
I thought of things both wild and rare.
Perhaps it was part of some device
For electrocuting mice,
Or of that strange machine
With a permanent distemper
That makes coffee in a temper.
Maybe t'was just a coil
For conveying lubricating oil.
And then he spoke.
Oh! What splendid illumination!
He volunteers this information:
"It's for a garden seat,
It protects the wood, you know, a treat."

SUNDAY

Sunday, the one day of the week
When I am at my ease.
When I can do just what I please.
When I can wander down lovely, lonely lanes
And be at pains to master what I will.
When I can be myself. for good or ill.

Sunday, the one day of the week
When I escape from the busy throng.
When I go wandering in the fields
And in some shady nook an old much loved book
I read, and strange fancy takes me by the hand
Into a new and ever changing land.

Sunday, the one day of the week
When I can climb the hills,
Explore the country any way
And be myself, come what may.
For what care I for shops and trade?
It's not for this that I was made.

Leave behind this buy and sell,
And wander where the heart would dwell.

THE SEAGULLS ASPIRATION

No low flying aircraft
No motor cars,
No air and sea pollution,
No inter-continental ballistic missile,
No atom bombs, no cruelty,
No slums, no wars.
No humans.
Peace.

Sammy Seagull

FOR CORDELIA

I have not thought much of success,
Of money or of happiness,
But just to wander with my kind
In secret ways within the mind.
With music, poetry, lovely things
That lift and spread the spirit's wings.

And finding there joy untold,
Have sought to share it, to unfold
My mind and heart to someone dear,
But none there were till she came near,

And I have ceased to wander long,
For all my joys with her belong.

FIVE HAPPY YEARS

Five happy years have sped away
Since that most dear, delighful day
When you and I together lay
In the meadow down by the river
And watched the skylark rise and fall,
The meadow grasses waving tall,
And heard the plover's plaintive call
In the meadow down by the river.

A narrow path ran through the grasses
Down to the bank where the river passes,
And now and then the kingfisher flashes
In the meadow down by the river.
And all day long we two lay,
No need for you or I to say
How blissful was that April day
In the meadow down by the river.

And every time I looked at you
I seemed to see the world anew,
And Oh! the days too quickly flew
All in the cloudless weather,
When every sky was wide and bright
And every day brought fresh delight
And lovely was each starlit night
With you and I together.

But lovelier still you came to be
In your most sweet simplicity
Than even then you were to me
In the meadow down by the river,
For you and I together spent
Such days of carefree merriment
That all our joys seemed heaven sent
Just you and I together.

Five happy years have soon gone by
And many more before us lie
Because beneath that April sky
We each found one another,
And every time I hold your hand
I feel you know and understand
The sadness of that lonely land
That now is gone for ever.

The lonely land where all folk roam
Who have not found a hearth and home.

THOUGHT FOR THE DAY

To have their daily dose of doom,
The people take the Morning Gloom,
The Sunday Screech, the Daily Wail.
No wonder they look sad and pale
And fail to see the shining sky,
The river gliding softly by
With sparkling waters stretching wide
And sunlight like a flame inside.
Oh! How our live grow less and less
Through harping on unhappiness,
And shrink to such a dismal size
Because we will not use our eyes.
How often do we fail to see
The kindness born of courtesy?
So put aside the world's wide woes
And see just how our garden grows,
What tender plant may need our care,
What soul to rescue from despair.

(Unfinished)

QUEER FISH

*Look to where the birds are wading
In the fret left by the tide's trespass.*

(*Photograph by Bill Shaw*)

QUEER FISH

There they are! Imprisoned
In glass and steel and chrome.
They've motored fifty miles from home
To see the sea.
He and she.
Dull and smug
With Sunday papers, car radio
And large brown rug.
Surrounded by possessions
But empty inside.
Bored and bewildered
And bursting with pride.

Turn away from these queer fish
In their waterless aquarium.

Look to where the birds are wading
In the fret left by the tide's trespass.
To the gold-green pools
Starfish and anemone garlanded.
Wander along the shore
Among the sea shells and the soft sand.
Go hand in hand with the morning's freshness
And the world's blue brightness.

People in cars are incarcerated. Forget them.
They've left only a pool of of oil behind.
Symbolic pool of the wilfully blind.

WONDER

When I was young long years ago
A world of wonder wrapped me round,
And in every simple thing
I saw a mystery profound.

Where e're I went in childhood's ways
A sense of wonder filled my days,
And things that now seem commonplace
Were full of tender joy and grace.

I saw a fish glide in a stream,
And wondered how that speckled thing
Could wander thus as in a dream.

I saw a rainbow in the sky
And wondered how its coloured band
Was ever captured in my eye.

I found a flower by the rough roadside
And watched its petals open wide,
And wondered why it lived and died.

I watched cloud shadows moving down
The valley sides and wondered at
The beauty of earth's silent tides.

Then I met a girl whose thoughts mirrored mine,
And in her dress she wore a simple celandine,
And I wondered how I'd ever lived
Before I made her mine.

The years have flown.
I wonder still at all things there be,
But Oh! the joy of all the love
That she has brought to me.

For wonder's good when we are young
And more when we are old,
But Oh! the love that lies between
Is more than can be told.

THINK OF ME

Think of me when I am far away,
Not sadly with a dull dismay,
But cheerfully,
And bring me
Closer than the light of day,
Closer than the nearest thing,
Nearer than breath
Or heartbeat,
On a wellspring of silent thought
That in its free and perfect form
Recalls my image.
And there you see me,
Distance gone away
And I beside you
Whether night or day

JELLYFISH

Jellyfish are nearly all water,
And yet they are alive and thrive
And grow in water.
Jellyfish are rather strange
And wonderful things
When you think about them.

Tenuous, trembling, living forms
Of water are jellyfish. Pink or
Electric blue, shot through and
Through with tiny nerves and
Ringed with stings.
Queer, pale pulsating, almost
Impalpable things are jellyfish,
Floating in the water.

But not when they're left
By the tide and dried by
The wind and the sun.
Jellyfish aren't strange
Or wonderful any more.
But just drab, decomposing
Scabs upon the sand.
For the land has no use
For jellyfish. Only the sea
Can make them floating and
Free and phosphorescent
To range over the ocean and be
Rather strange and wonderful once more.

THE MOTH

They talked on Peace
And how they valued the gift of life,
Hated war and all bitter human strife.

A little moth fluttered by his knee,
He bent and crushed it deliberately toward eternity.

This delicate thing,
With myriad scales on dappled wing
Meant no more to him
Than stone or bead.
Such thoughtlessness is poverty indeed.

This little moth held such a world of wonder
That had he spent a lifetime in the search
He would have become so very wise
The universe - no less - would lay before his eyes.

But he made only a smudge upon his knee

ARCTIC TERN

From Pole to Pole
This slight feathered thing
Has cleaved the air
On tireless beating wing.
Has circled half the world,
Finding Antarctic skies
And southern summer seas.
On countless cycles of the sun
This journey ended and begun,
Venturing southward
Through many a thousand mile,
When man was only cradled
By the land-locked Nile.

BUMBLE BEE ON CROCUS

Lone voyager this fine March day,
A bumble bee has flown my way.
Now on his wide horizon looms
My window box of crocus blooms.
See! How he dives to share
The pollen-scented crocus fare,
Now climbing in, now coming out
With pollened feet and dew-drenched snout.
Within those purple caves what sights,
What flower-flavoured strange delights,
What tastes to tease that testing tongue,
And golden grains to spy upon!
When there, what paradise in view
Alone with stores of honey-dew!

ANTARCTICA OBSERVED

*(For A.G.E.Jones on the publication of
his first full length book in 1982)*

These facts lay scattered, lost, obscure,
And where to find them none were sure,
But now within these covers find
The author's journey of the mind,
To lay beside the reader's hand,
The story of this last-found land.
A journey made with skill and care,
By one who would no effort spare
To find the truth, where e'er it lay
In documents of yesterday.
Who never shirked a toilsome task,
But at the end would only ask
That those who followed in his way
Should due acknowledgment display.
Not to gain the public eye,
Or vanity to satisfy,
But just to keep the record straight
For searchers of a later date.

THE MUSEUM MOUSE

(After a series of many false call-outs from the local Museum to the Police, it was found that mice had chewed the alarm cable.)

The museum mouse was very wise
With silky coat and shiny eyes,
Which owed their bright illumination
To meals of plastic insulation.
But Mrs Mouse had oft observed
Their cosy meals were much disturbed
By noisy bells and burly men
Who came into their antique den
Just when the meal had seemed the best,
Destroyed their gastronomic zest.
The police declared this queer alarm
Did few much good and many harm,
Disturbed the sergeant's quiet repose
And wrecked the station's midnight doze.
So up they got, and all declared
That future calls would not be heard.
And mice and men are all agreed
Of false alarms they had no need,
That they would rather take to crime
Than be disturbed from time to time
By ghostly burglars in the night
Who gave them such a fearful fright.
Men came, and altered wires and bells,
The police retired to their cells
And mice found other things to chew,
Like books and cord and woodwork too,
Finding a doll's Victorian house
The very thing to house a mouse!

MONTY

Monty was an orphan cat,
His mother was run over.
He left the farm where he was born
And landed up in clover.

He left scant meals and bread and milk
And came to meat and fish,
And now he's twice the cat he was
From many a dainty dish.

His purr is wise and very fine,
His eyes are wise and knowing,
His tail is ringed and silky-fine,
His chest all white and snowy.

He loves to sleep in the old armchair,
He'll lie for hours and never stir,
But when he hears the fridge door click
He's wide awake in half a tick.

He loves to roam about at night
And set the roosting birds to flight.
But come the dawn he's on the sill
Ready to take his morning fill.

THE LOST MEADOW

There's a little meadow on the edge of town
Near the railway, where the lines run down,
Across a stone-built bridge and a shady pond,
With newts and duckweed and tall fern frond,
Where we played for whole long summer days
In a world of quiet, sequestered ways.

An occasional friendly, steaming train
Would come up the line and then down again.
Motor cars were few in number,
An aeroplane a thing of wonder,
And noise a distant, murmuring sound
That told you the world was still around.

But now the earth-grab tears with savage claws
And eats up the land with avid jaws.
The meadow is gone, the soil laid bare,
The pond filled in, the rails not there.
Only a stony track remains
Where the bright steel lines brought the railway
trains.

The sheltering barn with its dusty air,
Where the sunlight came through the window
square,
Has roof-timbers broken like splintered bones,
With only nettles among its stones.
And soon a housing estate will arise;
Another sweep of grassland dies.

Squat houses come, and TV masts,
But no trees for shelter from winter blasts.
No trees to sweeten the summer days,
To stand in the sky through the autum haze.
Now concrete will spread its lifeless load
Over the land where the cattle strode.

Over the path to the old barn door,
Where never a child will shelter more.
Cars will be parked the whole day through
And probably most of the night time too.
Then we shall long for our meadow again,
Wide to the sky and the wind and the rain.

The meadow that's gone beyond recall,
For a concrete wilderness covers it all.
And so it is when a meadow dies.
The life of the land defeated lies,
And we have made a desert place
Where green things grew by God's good grace.

TRASH

A bundle of feathers and string
And many a hidden, precious thing
Collected on the holiday.
What fun and play these simple things
Borne far and wide
On fancy's wings
Meant for the small boy.
Now homeward bound,
And to his father trusting brings
His treasures,
Seeking to keep inviolate
These tokens of his happy state.
For who can tell
What here in lies
Behind the child's
Unsullied eyes?

"No room for trash,
Throw them away!"
With these harsh words
The vision fades,
See through his tears
The child obey.

The boy no longer seaward wades,
No longer plays upon the sand,
Lost in a far-off feathered land.
Gone is the romance of the string
That circumscribed
A magic ring.

For a mean backyard
Mid City Grime
Could have been a sea beach anytime,
With many a seabird wandering wide
Beyond the fast receding tide.

Fine castles fashioned in the sand
By lordly kings and ladies grand
Have pennants floating brave and fair,
made from the "Trash" abandoned there.
Alas! This day dream fades and dies.
And one small boy with tear-dimmed eyes,
Goes homeward under cloud filled skies.
One sore heart, featherless and forlorn,
Is left a secret loss to mourn.

But how much more the man should grieve
Who thus obscured
A world of make-believe?

SUNLIGHT

Out at sea a breaker catches the sunlight,
Why does my heart leap at such a sight?
Inside there are hidden reservoirs of beauty

Where sunlight sparkles on moving water
And shines through green leaves
Within grateful solitudes.
Herein lies the secret of one's whole attitude to life.
One need not feel the day's despair
If one has beauty hidden there.

DREAMS

Since childhood days
I have dreamed many dreams.
Conquests of the mind
That I would make.
Some inner urge has led me to forsake
The common highway,
And wander in the by-way of the spirit's longing.
Though all has come to naught,
And the telling of it is a weary tale,
Yet we will not despair.
For it was a fair vision
And well worth the having.
And though the world sees no success.
She who is my happiness and all my living
Knows the inner vision and the spirit's longing
She to me, and I to her belonging.

LACE

Sometimes the sea
Leaves lace-like patterns
Gently undulating
Laid on the sea's surface.
Countlessly
From primeval times
Before man's eyes
Had opened in wide surprise
At the world's wonders,
These lace-like patterns
Have come and gone,
And who knows what
Mysterious and hidden loom
Such things are fashioned on?

Sometimes the clouds
Spread out in wave-like forms,
And fill the sky with beauty,
In solemn procession we see them go.
Their slow majesty
Is like a benediction.
As we lie
Tall grasses wave
Against the sky.
Since the round earth
And its waters were,
These forms have fashioned
In the silent air.

ROOKS NESTING

The rooks are building once again
In the high trees
Down the lane,
As often they have done before.
I remember year by year
Since childhood days
Their boisterous ways.
                Caw-Caw -
Black forms like shapes of night
Or burnt paper
                Taken flight.
Like outstretched hands
Against the sky,
Coming with twigs and sticks
                And straw
Like flotsam on a windswept shore.
And how they fight and scuffle
In the trees.
                Noisy messengers,
Crying that winter's long travail
Is blossomed out in Spring again.
What comfort to the heart
                They bring.
That though men mar
And spoil the earth,
                These birds
At the call of the year's beginning,
Start their building.
The old life ending,
The new life bringing.

ROOKS NESTING

*The rooks are building once again
In the high trees down the lane.*

(*Photograph by Bill Shaw*)

MYSTERY

It has been said not long ago
That nature is not friend but foe.
But why should one who gave him birth
Be hostile to man's stay on earth?

If man upon the loom of life
Was woven out of cosmic strife,
Why should such creative skill
Be used to work for human ill?

No man knows from whence we came.
Are we some cosmic gambler's game?
Surely this can never be
A vast and pointless lottery.

Man looks beyond his own brief span
And tries to see creation's plan.
But why should child of Nature yearn
For knowledge he can never learn?

The fact that man looks far beyond
The confines of his earthly bond,
Would seem to show an inner light
Illumined by a mystic light.

THE WORLD

Although the world is open wide
And all can know who comes and goes,
Yet no one any better knows
Where flows the ceaseless tide.
'Knowing' all the world's affairs
Diminishes the simple mind,
Makes the sightless still more blind
And burdens them with cares.

I only wish a quiet mind
That looks out from a spirit free
And seeks its own identity
At one with its own kind

I would not dwell in an ivory tower
Or seek to walk in secret ways
But just to spend unhurried days
With many a fruitful hour.

Not caring for the false displays,
Happy to find the kindred folk,
Who oft times to the spirit spoke
In well remembered ways,

These are the friends that I would prize
And cherish all my life long through,
Not caring how the world might view
Through dis-enchanted eyes.

For most that nurtures human life
And for mankind the future holds,
Is what the gifted mind unfolds
Despite men's greed and strife.

THE SEA IS NOT FOR SALE

The sea is not for sale
Nor the beauty of a pale
Spring morning.
Or any day's dawning
That brings delight.
Nor any night
That with its restful sleep
Enfolds the ceaseless world
In quiet solitude.
Such things cannot be
Bought or sold.
Whether we are young or old,
We can but breathe a thankful prayer
That kindly Providence, despite despair,
Gives such moments to gaze
Into the heart of beauty
And know her ways.

THE ARTIST

The artist ever
Seeks to span
The world of nature
And of man,
To capture all
That passes by
With ready hand
And ardent eye.

Forever linked
To sea and sky
To fields and forest
Plain and glade
To face and form
In man and maid,
Yet seldom daunted
Or dismayed.

He does not look
With careless gaze
Upon the scenes
That fill his days
But seeing beyond
The commonplace
Invests it with
A special grace,
This gives his life
A purposed air
And banishes
The day's despair.

THE MUSE

The shallow line can only show
What emptiness exists below,
And pompousness begets a screed
Of rapid growth, though lifeless seed,
And word on word keeps rolling round
The empty barrel's hollow sound.
And so we come to near despair
Through words that fall on unquiet air.

So much bad prose as poetry dressed
Must surely stir the Muse's rest,
And make her dreams like nightmares styled,
Who lived with Keats and Blake beguiled,
Stayed summer days by Shakespeare's side,
With Tennyson would often ride,
Through Donne and Wordsworth spanned the years
With poetry full of joy and tears.

But now she dwells in toneless times,
Who once was lulled by faultless rhymes.
And only Pitter joyful brings
New music from the lyre's strings.
She alone this latter day
Brings forth the muse both sad and gay,
And with her merry minstrel's air
Makes music for the world to share.

POEM ON A POEM

The words must lie on the quiet page
And fall from the lips like honey-dew,
And shine in the mind like the evening star
Whether they be many or few.
The thoughts must flow like a murmuring stream
And dwell in the mind with an easy grace
And shine in the heart that gives them rest
Like the smile on a beautiful face.

LINES TO A YOUNG POET

Your poems are too simple and direct.
You must strive to be more obscure
And less correct,
To deal in involutions and diverse confusions,
Speak of loos, graffiti, and such like things.
Take refuge in intellectual constructions
That are only pimply cerebral eruptions.
Say all the world is ugly and unfair.
Above all, never have rhyme or reason,
That would be tantamount to treason!

POETS' PUB

Poets in pubs to me seem queer,
A spurious culture spawned by beer,
A counterfeit of bonne homme
That cuts no ice with such as me.
For alcoholic stimuli
Breeds the furtive fuddled lie,
And talk that circulates with booze
Is either sport or sex or news.
For poetry's in an alien place
When mirrored in the barmaid's face,
And private thoughts matured in rhyme,
Belong to quite a different clime.

POEMS

Poems are private things
Meant for the inner ear.
To speak them in the market place
Brings a sadness I fear.
Yet sometimes from out the crowd
Shines a face of delight,
A moment of contact
Dispels a wilderness of night.

TO A FRIEND IN DEEP DISTRESS

The world has suddenly changed,
And you who cared so deeply
Are now estranged
From all around.
Oh! So steeply stretches out
The weary road
That you must climb.
But all the love and deep concern
That you have shown
Still lives within your heart,
And those whom you have known
Had lives made richer
For the part you played,
And this can never be discounted,
Nor to a final end be brought.
For it was a noble thing,
So finely wrought
Of tenderness, compassion, love
And deep concern.
And in times and places that we do not know
Its light shall shine and all its beauty glow.

UNKNOWN LAND

The simplest thing that comes to hand,
The very tiniest grain of sand,
Reveals a vast and unknown land
When we would seek to understand.
So how can we ever hope to see
Into the secrets of eternity?

Man may probe and analyse,
And measure out the earth and skies,
But he will never stand before
The secret heart, the inmost core.
The mind that brings him inner light
Yet has its own perpetual night.

Shall we despair that what man knows
Is only as the wind that blows,
And all his knowledge but a spark
That throws a glimmer in the dark?
Or shall we with humility have faith,
Where knowledge cannot see?

ALONE

We wander through the world alone,
And call not anyone our own,
For even loved ones seldom see
Into the heart's deep mystery.
In moments rare the veil grows thin,
We feel that we may enter in
But then the world's coarse voice intrudes.
Sometimes a voice, a kindly smile
Will banish loneliness awhile,
The friendly word, the gentle voice
Oft times can make the heart rejoice.
Remember well these moments rare
When love alone defeats despair,
The pattern of our life should be
Guided by this simplicity,
Remember this, where e'er you be
And walk with true humility.

TO A FRIEND

To keep inward peace
Preserve outward calm,
Bend to the wind of words
And come to no harm.
Be quiet often,
Look in the mirror of the mind,
See there your soul
And be not blind.
The world has many ways,
Tread but your own,
Be true to that,
T'is for you alone.
This you have done
As well I know,
Friends of the mind
Are ever so.

REALITY

Man has reached out for the moon
And now arrived there all too soon,
And so to Mars and Venus probe
Then leave behind this tiny globe.
But himself he cannot leave behind
He is the prisoner of his mind.

However far man ventures wide
He never can escape outside
The inner world of life and mind,
That life so real and well defined
Of things to touch and things to see, -
The only true reality.

THE LONELY

In all the world there is no love
Like the love of a lonely lass.
For the love of a lonely lass is sure
And wells from a spring that is deep and pure
And has the power to flow and endure
Whatever the day may be.

In all the world there is no love
Like the love of a lonely lad.
For the love of a lonely lad is kind
And has the power to hold and bind
And flood in light where all was blind,
Whatever the day might be.

In all the world there is no love
Like the love of the lonely ones,
For when man and maid their love discover
Each one loved, each one a lover,
Then they a world of wonder uncover,
And care not what the day may be.

THE CAVE

Human thought can travel far
Out and beyond the farthest star,
And yet is tied to living flesh.
Captured within a tremulous mesh
Encapsulated in a bony cave
Where dwells a fool, a saint, a knave.

The words that lie upon this page
Are transcripts from a hermitage,
And they have come by devious ways
Through long forgotten lonely days,
Into the cave where dwells the man
The stars have made since worlds began.

And when his little time is past,
The cave made empty at the last,
These words, still laid upon the page,
Will be another's heritage
And to another spirit call
Though laid so silent and so small.

THE QUEST

I stand in a moment of time,
That time has, - gone, -gone, -gone
I am linked to the world's turning
And the stars burning.
How?
Is my clock of consciousness wound
When the sperm pierces the cell?
There is my personal heaven or hell
Made, and I am not asked to be born,
I cannot be asked, for this is my dawn
In the dim world of pre-conscious living
In the life that gives me life.

We show only vaguely what went before
And not at all what comes after,
Our life is made of grains of gladness
And seasons of sorrow,
With cares of the day
And thoughts of the morrow.
If we can laugh and make others laugh
Then we are in a moment of time joyful.   (Unfinished)

SMOKE SCREEN

Men with pipes look so absurd.
They really do, upon my word!
Standing there, owlish, wise,
Especially in their own eyes.
In tube and bus and cinema
They fill the air with dilute tar.
With cigarettes they're even worse,
If possible, a greater curse.
So why this widespread addiction
To such an obvious affliction?
Combustible dummy tits must soothe the boy
Or be a kind of grown-up toy,
A mark of having reached the stage
When he becomes a masculine sage,
And lords it in the pub at nights,
On politics and boxing fights,
Or how he dated several birds
And with the foreman had some words!

A kind of comfort to the mind?
Or a smoke screen to hide behind?

RHYME FOR A BEER MAT

Beer in a never ending stream
Flows through the human ditch,
It dulls the brain
And blocks the drain
And makes the brewers rich.

THE DERELICT DOOR

The derelict door stands grim and grey,
And no one comes here night or day
Where once the busy housewife cleaned,
Where white steps shone and handle gleamed,
Where paintwork, smooth and clean, displayed
The burnished knocker full arrayed,
With letter box and handle bright
Shining and smart in the morning light.
But now the step is dark below,
The knocker never gives a blow,
The handle rusty, useless, bent,
That once was such an ornament
Is now forlorn and quite forsaken,
And nothing more can now awaken
The silent derelict door,
Or bring back the life it knew before.
For the paintwork flakes in dust and blisters,
Across the threshold a snall-trail glisters.
Cobwebs stretch in the corner space
And over the door the spiders race.
Through the keyhole the wandering air
Moves down the passage so dismal and bare,
And seeks for answers to moans and sighs,

THE DERELICT DOOR   *And make the doorway, for a whole*
summer day. A world of enchanted
and wonderful play.

(Photograph by F.M. Sutcliffe)

But the empty house never replies.
No laughter or sorrow, no sadness or joys
No child to play with dollies and toys
And make the doorway, for a whole summer day,
A world of enchanted and wonderful play.
Only a leaf in the cobweb there
Plays in the moving current of air.

THE HOUSE

I saw a house today, so still
I thought its inmates must be ill,
So silent and forlorn,
Its windows eyeless, its steps so worn,
A most abandoned place
Wearing the aspect of a careworn face,
Bereft of joy and inward grace.
      * * *   * * *

I wrote these lines some time before
I saw that closed and friendless door.

A strange presentiment it seems,
Uncertain light that fitful gleams.

What brought this house before my mind,
Before I saw its aspect blind?

I cannot tell; may never know,
I only know that it is so.

THE LOVERS

There was a maid so sweet and so fair,
She went into a bluebell wood
And met her only lover there,
All things betwixt them understood.

The spirit of the wood that day
Being abroad in curious mood,
Watched the lovers as they lay
And saw them as they wooed.

And he grew jealous of their love,
Wished that he might be as they,
And drew some vapours from above
Upon them as they lay.

The vapours wrapped them both around,
And they were gone from mortal eye,
For they have never more been found
And yet they did not die.

Each spring the flowers come and go,
Each summer do they pass,
And nature knows that this is so
With a lover and his lass.

Her cheeks are as the roses red
And eglantine her hair,
And mossy is her bridal bed
As she is lying there.

For thoughts he takes the pale moonbeams,
For smiles the light of day,
And laughter is the running stream
Where they together play.

GORSE

*(Remembering Linnaeus, who fell on his
knees before the gorse.)*

Thank God for golden gorse
On the open moors,
And great clouds
That throw moving shadows
On the earth,
And all living things
That give birth to life and beauty,
Clear moorland streams,
The wind that blows the heather,
Life giving rains,
Sunshine, and all that remains
Of wonder and of joy
In man and boy.

NATURAL THINGS

Natural things give such delight,
They keep the spirit clear and bright.

Dewdrops on green leaves laid
By morning light displayed.

Sunshine on a fresh spring day
That makes the heart so light and gay.

A rainbow after storm and thunder,
A thing of beauty and of wonder.

The solitary walk; the sweet daydream;
The murmuring voice of a moorland stream.

Daffodils and April skies
That fill the heart with glad surprise.

Sunlight and shadow beneath tall trees;
An upland meadow in a gentle breeze.

Clear truth seen in splendid eyes;
The glorious spread of a bright sunrise.

Drought ended by sweet rain
That lets you live and breath again.

To me all these and much untold
More precious are than finest gold.

THE MOSS

The moss that lives on the old grey stone
Knows but itself alone,
And takes no living thing to task.
Nor does it ever ask
Of God a favour,
But lives green-velveted and close cemented,
Serene and mossy well contented.
If we would learn from little mosses
We'd know the truth of gains and losses.

A GIFT OF ROSES

Your roses gave me untold pleasure,
To me they're like a hidden treasure
Discovered in a secret place
By smiling Fortune's special grace.
To think these sticks in winter time
Are coated with a frosted rime
That now in blaze of red and gold,
The alchemy of Earth unfold.
But best of all a friendly call
Transforms into a festival.

A LITTLE GARDEN

I know a little garden
So peaceful and so fair,
And someone very dear to me
Who works and wanders there,
And where there is no room
For sadness or despair.

For a robin sings in the twilight,
And a blackbird in the dawn,
High up in the rowan tree
Or down by the thickset thorn,
And a little pool mirrors the stars
Till another day is born.

But though a thousand nights should come
And a thousand days should go,
My love is ever dear to me,
More dear I could not know,
And even were it possible
I should not wish it so.

POPPIES

The sheltering hedge
Lay in between
The motor road
And the field of green,
And there we found
To our delight
Clusters of poppies
Glowing bright.
This random harvest
Will not stir
The faintest breath
In mart or fair.
But who should talk
Of price or pay
When gifts of beauty
Come their way?

SNAPDRAGONS ON GARDEN WALL (self-seeded)

Each year they come,
Grown on the wall.
How do they grow on stone
So tall?
They ask little of life
Just a crevice in stone.
Oh! But the sun and the rain
They call their own.
Seen through my window pane
They dance in the sun,
They sing in the rain.
Though silent their song
It is here in my heart.
Praise be to God
For the joy they impart.

77

THE DAISY

Simple daisy growing wild,
Flower of the little child.
How I love your tiny face
Full of tender joy and grace.

In the early morning dew
You wash your golden face anew,
Waiting for the coming light
Before you open wide and bright.

Such wonder lies within your gold,
The all of it was never told.
The wisest man can only be
A little child in face of thee.

WROUGHT IRON GATES

You were born of strong hands
And fierce fires,
Yet have delicate tracery
Spread like bare branches
Against the winter sky.
The hand and eye that fashioned you
Had sure dexterity
And a perfect view
Of what the thing should be,
Such as only poets and saints
And craftsmen see.

BOOKWORM

I used to be a bookworm,
But that was long ago,
Now my sight grows rather dim
And books I must forgo.
Most every day just after tea
I'd with my books be found,
And never knew what time it was
Till time for bed came round,
And even then beneath the sheets
I'd read away all night.
It's not a bit of wonder
I've ruined of my sight.
But never mind
I've come out top!
They say the worm will turn,
I've ceased to be a bookworm,
The midnight oil to burn,
Instead I am a tapeworm
With casettes by the score
And Calibre look after me
As I've never been before!

COMMONDALE MOOR

Thank Goodness for
Rosebay willow herb,
Dry stone walls,
The brown runnels
Where the winter rills
Run valleywards.
And the calm contours of
The quiet hills,
Here on the high moor
The peace and the pure
Air are a benediction.
We are quite happy here,
We two.
A simple meal and such a view,
Is all we have, save our at-oneness
With each other and the world.
So the meal, the moor,
The distant hills, the air,
The stream, the sky, the earth,
Are made a paradise,
An Eden in the first beginning.
A miracle from us two springing.
Having no source save we,
Who gave it birth.

JAMES CLARK ROSS

*(For Admiral M.J. Ross on the publication of his
book, Ross in the Antarctic, 1982)*

A century or more ago
Great-grandpa sailed to the southern seas,
Beyond the rim of the world he went
To the grey and ghastly antipodes,
And there he found - Oh! wondrous sight -
A mountain glowing in the night,
An icy barrier huge and strange,
And far beyond, a mountain range.
All this - where others gone before
Had only glimpsed a distant shore,
Uncertain rock or icy spur.
So we, with truth may well infer
He was the first beyond dissent
To find the Antarctic continent,
And threading lines through frosty air
To find the polar magnet's lair,
Completing in these southern times
His earlier work in northern climes.
Three voyages made he in these years
And swept aside all doubts and fears.
Bending those beneath his sway
In his firm, courageous way.
And though a distant, lonely man,
As all must be who work and plan
Endeavours on so large a scale,
Yet now he stands, for all to see
Unrivalled in his victory.

DYING

Dying means parting with time.
How we walk our timeless way
We do not know,
But when the call comes
We must go.

There is no return
The way is an endless track,
No one has ever found
The road back.

If it be not in time
Nor yet in space
How can we tell
Of such a formless place?

There is no motion, no light,
No conscious I.
How shall we know
When we do die?

Others will know,
Perhaps regret we have gone,
But they must be timeless too,
Yes, every one.

Sleep is a timeless place,
Then we awaken to the dawn.
Is death a timeless sleep
Then we are re-born?

If it be so,
Then all is not lost.
We must go on
And count not the cost

If oblivion awaits
Then life is most strange,
A pointless endeavour
We are powerless to change.

LAKE SIDE MUSINGS

The glowing light of eventide
Spreads gently over waters wide,
Black branches hanging low
Seem tunnels to the depths below,
And all around the glimmering lake
The silent forms of night awake
The voiceless world that lies around
And yet inside my brain is found.
It is so real, though far from man,
So far the mind can ever span,
And yet these thoughts are of it all
And can to memory's eye recall
This scene where ever we may be.
A fragment of eternity?   (Unfinished)

THE TARN

The moorland tarn lay clear and bright
The day was one of calm delight
With only distant figures seen
Across the moor that lay between.
The tranquil solitude was sweet
So different from our busy street
No sound of cars - no strident voice
Only the swallows here rejoice
And dragonflies with glistening wing
Like lords of light come hovering.
We two were filled with sweet content
As bees in heather came and went
Murmuring through the moorland haze
Their pollen-scented secret ways,
And waterfowl all unafraid
Among the reeds and rushes wade
Or make their arrow-angled wake
Across the tiny moorland lake

THE WOOD

I once went a walk
Into a wood - Oh
It was good to wander
Under the great green canopy.
To watch the foilage moving
Over the earth and the grasses
Sun shown and wind wavered.
A splendid, spacious, sun-filled
Leaf embowered cathedral.
Grown silently out of the earth
Through many centuries.
More lovely than any built
By man. Built imperceptibly
Inch by inch to span the air,
With rain and rough winds,
Snow and silent frosts,
And aisles of shafted sunlight.

THE RUINED MILL

Down a leaf-lined lane where time stands still
Lies a waterfall and a ruined mill.
Tall fern fronds fill the hedgerows there
And meadowsweet foams in the fragrant air.
Round the ruin the trees grow tall
Where the long lane ends by the waterfall.

Here the old mill crumbles away
Through the starlit night and the long lone day.
Crumbles away in the grey green shade
The trees, the ferns and the weeds have made.
Crumbles away in the cold grey dawn
'Mid bramble thicket and thickset thorn.

Crumbles away by the old mill race
Where the stream spreads out in a marshy
place.
And never a cart is seen in the lane,
Never a load of golden grain,
And the millstone lies half buried below
Where once the mill stream used to flow.

Yet sometimes on a moonless night
The mill wheels turn and the mill lamps light,
The wheels of a cart sound in the lane,
The voice of the miller is heard again
Hailing the farmer as he rounds the bend
With his load of grain at the long lane's end.

THE RUINED MILL   *Round the ruin the trees grow tall*
Where the long lane ends by the
waterfall.

(Photograph by F.M. Sutcliffe)

But morning light brings the cold grey dawn,
For only in dreams is the mill re-born,
Only in dreams do the mill lamps burn,
Only in dreams does the miller return.
So let us dream of our water mill
Down a leaf-lined lane where time stands still.

EPISCOPAL VISIT

My Lord Archbishop comes today
The dignity of high office to display,
An office rare and most refined
To which archbishops are inclined.
Aye - and here comes the rub,
To wit, the opening of a pub.
It seems beyond belief, I know,
Yet I assure you it is so.

THE GREAT PUBLIC HOUSES

This way to see the tapestries,
That way to see the chairs,
To the left to find the costumes,
The portraits are up the stairs.
Thirty p. to get into the zoo,
The armour and weapons are all on view,
And if you would see some folios rare
Find the library and linger there.
But if some refreshment you would take
You will find the cafe beside the lake,
And if you come from the U.S.A.
You can sleep in the four-poster and stay for the day -
It only costs you ninety pounds
Including a splendid tour of the grounds.
The Duchess will most affably smile,
The Duke will accompany you in style,
Their daughters will grace the evening meal
And your cheque book will have the greatest appeal.
For this was once a stately home
But now the public can through it roam,
And what was once a quiet retreat
Is now as busy as a London street.
All must now these treasures share,
Have money and culture and time to spare,
Not just the cream at the top of the pot,
But the curds and the whey, the milk and the lot.
So buy your tickets and take your fill.
The aristocrats are top of the bill!

A LITTLE BIT OF NONSENSE

OPTICAL DELUSIONS
(With apologies to Lewis Carol)

He thought he saw a crocodile
Laid upon a log.
He looked again and saw it was
A tail without a dog.
"It's strange," he said, "the things you see
When looking through a fog."

He thought he saw an omnibus
Parked inside a zoo.
He looked again and saw it was
A python eating glue.
"That's really very strange," he said
"It's not what reptiles do."

He thought he saw a large giraffe
Reclining on a bed.
He looked again and saw it was
The Canon Featherhead.
"I'm awfully sorry, sir," he said
"To make your face so red."

He thought he saw a tabby cat
Sitting on a wall.
He looked again and saw it was
A bounce without a ball.
"I mustn't look again," he said,
"It wouldn't do at all."

The moral of this dreadful tale
Is very plain indeed.
It is that what you think you see
May very well not be,
And what seems obvious to you
May not be so to me.

THE GOURMET

I like sausage rolls made with nails and glue,
They're very good for indigestion
If you know just what to do,
You peg them on a washing line
And wait a week or two.

I like rissoles mixed with light brown ale,
You stir them up for weeks and weeks
In a large enamel pail,
And then you pour it down the sink
In case your spirits fail.

I like buns made with screws and old grey socks,
They're very good if mixed up well
And baked on sun-kissed rocks.
They'll cure your gout and other ills
Including chicken-pox.

I like sweet cakes mixed with coloured paints,
They're excellent for choir boys,
They make them look like saints,
But not so good for organists,
They subject them to faints.

91

GREEN SKY

I wonder if the sky were green
And if the grass were blue
And we walked about upon our heads,
We'd see a different view?
Or if by being upside down
We'd take it all as true?

I wonder if we slept all day
And walked about at night,
We'd think the moon was like the sun
And also black was white?
Or if by being wide awake,
We'd think it all quite right.

I wonder if the sea was dry
And all the land was wet
And we sailed about from town to town
With every port to let,
Then what would jolly Jack Tar do
And the fisherman with his net?

THE MARROW
(with apologies to Longfellow)

I shot a marrow in the air
It fell to earth in Berkeley Square
The nightingales all gathered round
And wondered what had hit the ground.

One said it was a strange balloon
Another said "a legless loon"
But all agreed it was most weird
The way the thing had just appeared.

The cook who lived at number nine
Said: "That's a marrow and it's mine."
But all the nightingales concurred
In what he said they hadn't heard.

They built their nests around its rim
And paid not any heed to him
And when the fledglings flew about
They sang upon his water spout.

EPIGRAMS

Little worm curled so neat,
If only you had useful feet,
You would get more swiftly round
And by the birds would not be found.

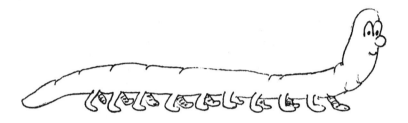

Let cold be cold and hot be hot,
And do not care one little jot,
For if you care for things so small
You will not have a life at all.

* * *   * * *

Sums are such an awful bore,
For why should two and two make four?
If two and two made twenty-three
We'd have more money for a spree!

* * *   * * *

Tell me, little parasite
Why you're eating day and night.
If you only stopped to think it out,
You'd find you shouldn't be about.

* * *   * * *

I'm not a D.J. Fan
Nor a disco habituee.
I'm not a grand old man
Nor an ordinary O.A.P.
I'm just a middle-aged in-between
And nobody thinks of me.

* * *   * * *

I love Keats and Shelley,
Raphael and Botticelli,
But have no use for Henry Moore.
He might go well in Thailand
But better still in Easter Island.

ON AN ORNATE MEMORIAL

What paragon of all the virtues she,
Who, though entombed,
Speaks out to you and me?
Loving and kind,
A wife and mother
So perfect,
No catalogue of praise
Could discover.
Can such a eulogy be really true
Or was she in reality
A shrew?

HOLY ISLAND

When the tide flows round the Holy Isle
Then peace descends for a little while.
In shells and stones and rocks and air
The saints of old dwell everywhere,
But when the tide flows back from the land
The crowds invade like a conquering hand.
The venomous mead has faintest touch of honey,
But lots and lots of greed-gained money,
And only Bingo and Amusements we need
To grace the Isle of the Venerable Bede.

But courage, Friends!
The tide still flows . . . . !

GOLF

Look out over the golf course,
I bet there's someone at play.
No matter if fog is thick on the ground,
There's sure to be someone
Playing a round.
Only six feet of snow will keep them away,
And then, you see,
They collect at the clubhouse bar,
To tell the world
How clever they are,
Without a doubt,
To knock such a tiny ball about.

THE PAINTER

There's an empty house across the road,
At least the upper rooms are bare,
But the lower ones have a painter there.
He keeps his paints and brushes and trestles.
And on a shelf quite innocent nestles
A bottle marked 'Turpentine'
Which holds a rare and vintage wine . . .

(Unfinished)

MOTOR CAR

The motor car was made for those
Who have no ears nor any nose.
The motor car was made to slay
So many people every day.
The aeroplane was made to fly
Tired executives through the sky,
And military criminals to smile
At human bodies pile on pile.
If men could master car and plane
To work for joy and not for gain,
If men could master fierce desire
Where power in wealth and greed aspire
To use men's bodies and their minds . . . .(unfinished)

THE SEARCH

I sought a way by intense application,
But no way has been found.
I have thought long and pondered,
And have heard but an empty sound.

I have gone into quiet places and sought rest,
But only my troubled heart beats in my breast.

I have travelled far and been in every place,
And always come back to see my own face.

I have read philosophers and wise men,
But have seen no light.
I have consulted my friends and overheard my enemies,
Yet no one has set me right.

I went into crowds and sought the company of my kind,
Yet all was in vain and none did I find.

Then I turned my steps homewards and found it was there,
The end of my searching, the answer to prayer.

JUST A THOUGHT

The city glare of noise and light
Shuts out the world of stars from sight,
The aeroplane and motor car
Have left upon man's soul a scar,
And thoughtless men pollution spread,-
Which circulates when they are dead-
To compass some immediate gain
At cost of future loss and pain.
All this I know and do deplore,
And much beside that men ignore,
But sorrow at man's wayward ways
Will never lighten lonely days;
And so I leave you with the thought
That sunshine can't be sold or bought,
That little children often smile
And puppies wag their tails awhile,
That laughter lifts a load of care
And courage carries off despair,
And though the world so wayward seems
Yet men find solace in their dreams.

ACKNOWLEDGEMENTS

For permission to reproduce the Sutcliffe pictures we have to thank the Whitby Literary and Philosophical Society who own the Copyright and the Sutcliffe Gallery of Whitby. The other photographs are by Bill Shaw, another artist behind the camera lens, who also knows the unsung trials of editing and publishing. Edna Whelan has kindly designed the cover and several of the drawings. The others are by Sister Clare and Peter Freeman. I am most grateful to all these friends.